The Positive Guide to Anger Management

The Most Practical Guide on How to Be Calmer, Learn to Defeat Anger, Deal with Angry People, and Living a Life of Mental Wellness and Positivity

Richard Banks

GW00503217

Thank You!

Thank you for your purchase.

I am dedicated to making the most enriching and informational content. I hope it meets your expectations and you gain a lot from it.

Your comments and feedback are important to me because they help me to provide the best material possible. So, if you have any questions or concerns, please email me at richardbanks.books@gmail.com.

Again, thank you for your purchase.

INTRODUCTION

We're all familiar with anger. It's present inside us, and it almost seems to be part of our blood. But have you ever wondered why anger exists?

Anger is an entirely natural emotion. Often, when we're irate, the response from people around us lets us know it's not okay to be that angry. However, it becomes frustrating being told that anger isn't good, and only in finding the root cause can things get better. Unfortunately, there's no one cause for anger. Anger can be triggered inside us for various reasons.

It might arise when we feel rejected, unhappy, unloved, or generally irritated. Sometimes anger comes to the fore within us because things didn't go as we'd planned. Life is unpredictable, and it can give us many challenges.

Whatever happens in life or whatever challenges we face aren't always under our control because many of these are external factors.

There are two types of influences in our life—external and internal factors. External factors include things you see every day in your mirror—your facial features and your body. Internal factors are responsible for how your body works as a whole. This includes your organs and your internal systems. Without these, you wouldn't be able to move a single limb.

The most important organ in your body is your brain. There's a close relationship between your body and your mind. This is known as the mind-body connection. These two aspects function together so you can work as a whole being. When there's a positive influence internally, this impacts you externally. The opposite is also true because of the mind-body connection.

There are more internal than external factors that influence us, and these consist of your sensations, emotions, and soul. Internal factors include how you react to, deal with, and face things. Your emotions arise from your mind, and your mind is responsible for almost everything you do. When you reach for a glass of water, it might seem like this is a function of your body, but the movement is initiated in your mind. When you feel happy, sad, anxious, or scared, it's because your mind is signaling you to feel that way.

Anger is one of our emotions, and it happens because our brain signals us to respond in this way. For instance, say you worked hard at your workplace to get a bonus, but someone else got it.

You might feel angry because you didn't get the bonus even though you worked day and night to earn it. But can you change that reality? The reality can't be changed, but you can react to it differently. You might find out why you didn't get the bonus and work even harder next time to try to get it.

All these things demonstrate that we might not have control over whatever's happening outside, but there's one thing we *can* have control over— ourselves. We can control how we react to things.

We might not be able to control the external factors that trigger our anger response, but we can take control of our internal factors. Anger is a natural response to the threats we face in our life. The emotion of anger often makes our heart race as the result of adrenaline rushing through our body, and sometimes anger makes our muscles tighten up. Perhaps it's these physical responses that make us aware that we're experiencing anger.

The emotion of anger is inherited from our ancestors, just like our sense of fear. There can be various things that trigger it, but all of them have one thing in common: when we feel angry, there's always an external factor contributing to it.

Some people express anger because, during their early years, they weren't taught how to control and manage it. When we hold anger inside us for too long, it gains strength, and we often end up exploding. Holding your anger in isn't a good thing, nor is expressing too much anger. Then what's the middle ground?

The middle ground is how you deal with your anger. Do you regard it as your friend or your enemy? If you see it as an enemy, that can make you feel miserable. You may also feel that your anger is unrelenting, and you might never be able to manage it.

So, to manage your anger, you need to become

friends with it. You need to figure out why it gets triggered. You need to accept that it's a part of you, and you'll eventually be able to make peace with it because anger can also be beneficial for you. Anger can motivate you to do things; it can help you express whatever you're feeling on the inside; it can prevent people from walking over you all the time. Anger isn't destructive if you know how to manage it healthily and properly. Once you know how to manage your anger, you'll also feel a close connection with your soul.

This guide is meant to help you learn how to healthily manage your anger. You aren't alone in this journey and, when you reach the end of this guide, you'll be shocked to know the powers and wonders that your mind and body are capable of. The following chapters will guide you through all the components of anger. Read this book with an open mind, and remember that you can manage your anger healthily. So, without any further ado, let's begin!

CHAPTER 1- HOW OUR MIND AFFECTS OUR BODY

"What we think determines what happens to us, so if we want to change our lives, we need to stretch our minds." -- Wayne Dyer

Whenever we face a setback, we may become quickly disappointed in our life. We often wish that we had superpowers to deal with a situation or a magic wand that could solve everything for us. The thing is, the real power lies inside you. It's present in you, and it shows in everything you do. It's responsible for you being alive. The powerful weapon and the magic wand is your mind. Your mind is capable of doing wonders with your body.

Human beings have three aspects—physical, mental, and spiritual. We're more likely to be concerned about our physical self. For instance, if we gain weight, we start taking appropriate steps to reduce it. We make sure to eat healthily, and we exercise regularly to shed some pounds.

However, after a week or two, if we haven't lost any weight, we may become disappointed and, oftentimes, unmotivated. We stop our efforts to lose weight and go back to the old way we were living before. Why does that happen? It happens because we tend to care more about our physical attributes than we do our mind. Without making up our mind that we want to lose weight, we'll never be able to do it.

This is the power your mind holds on your body. It's deeply connected with it. If you have a healthy mind, you'll have a healthy body. We often don't take much care of our inner self because we can't see it. However, it shows in everything we do. If we're in a bad mood, we might throw tantrums. If we're exhausted mentally, we might not do well in our academics. Your mind is the controller of your body. You might not be able to control your mind entirely, but you can understand how it works. When you know how your mind works, you can achieve or overcome almost anything in your life.

Let's take a look at how our mind affects our life.

Mind Power

Mind power is the strongest power that you possess. When you combine your mind power with your imagination, you can build a path toward your future and success. However, the power of the mind can also create obstacles and setbacks. It all depends on your mindset.

The foundation of your mind is your thoughts. You need to combine your thoughts with your emotions and your focus. When you do this, your reality is impacted as a result. Everything that happens in your mind is related to your attitude, and your behavior is highly dependent on the repetitive thoughts your mind has throughout the day.

Thoughts and Emotions

Your mind consists of a cloud of your thoughts. These thoughts are like packets of energy. They can either be positive or negative. The problem is that our mind typically consists of more negative thoughts than positive ones. Fortunately, we can work with our brains to start thinking more positively.

Our emotions are equally important to us as our thoughts. We often underestimate the power that our emotions hold. We need to understand how our emotions affect us. Having or displaying emotion is often perceived as a sign of weakness, and expressing our emotions is often labeled as an "emotional display." This is a wrong perception because, when we suppress our emotions, they often build up and are expressed even more strongly. This is especially true of anger, which is one of the emotions that we commonly experience. It's essential to be aware of our emotions and thoughts because this awareness is the only way can we manage them properly and recognize when they start to control us.

If you have a hormonal imbalance in your body, this can prevent your brain from producing enough serotonin, which is the hormone responsible for happiness. Insufficient serotonin can lead to a weakened immune system and unnecessary stress. It's been proven through research that stress can decrease your lifespan. This is because, when you're stressed, the telomeres in your DNA shorten, and your telomeres are responsible for the proper functioning of your entire being. Terminal diseases such as cancer can also be caused by having too much stress. Repressed anger and poorly managed anger also contribute to unnecessary stress that can negatively affect your health.

Controlling Your Mind

Our brain is responsible for the way we do and perceive things in life. It's truly a complex organ. How your heart beats and how your fingers move are all controlled by your brain. It's also responsible for processing and controlling your emotions. The range of human emotions may not yet be clear; however, the origins of emotions in the mind are given a lot of weight in the scientific world.

We aren't always taught how to control our thoughts. This is why our thoughts can feel like the enemy. We create negative thoughts and patterns and once these become a part of us, it takes time to shift from this old way of thinking.

The Parts of the Brain Responsible for Emotions

Your brain has a distinct area that's responsible for your emotions and your behavior. This is known as the limbic system. Your limbic system consists of the following:

Amygdala

This part of the brain helps with coordination as well as creating responses to how we react to events in our life. It's also the part of the brain that's triggered to generate emotions. This structure is where anger and fear originate.

Hypothalamus

This is the part of the brain that controls emotional responses. It also helps regulate body temperature, release of hormones, and sexual responses.

Limbic Cortex

This part of the brain consists of the parahippocampal gyrus and cingulate gyrus. It's responsible for our judgments, moods, and motivation.

Hippocampus

This is the part of our brain that deals with learning and memory formation.

The above is a brief and basic explanation of the origins of your emotions. Our primary focus is on anger, so let's take a look at how anger is controlled by our brain.

<u>The Evolution of Anger</u>

When you're in a situation that feels like a threat, you get angry. This tells us that anger is our brain's response when we face a stressor in our environment. Anger originates in the amygdala, which then stimulates the hypothalamus.

Certain parts of your prefrontal cortex also play a role in anger. This impacts how you express your emotions. Although the anger response is present in our DNA—which means we inherited it from our ancestors—have you ever wondered what coping mechanism they adopted to overcome anger?

Natural Survival Mechanism

Survival is the most basic mechanism of evolution. Every organism is adapted to its environment. The more adapted an organism is to its environment, the greater the chance of its survival. Adaptation is the behavioral characteristic that helps an organism to survive and live fully.

Historically, human beings have survived and adapted to many changing shifts in the environment, and this is because of their survival mechanism. We can still use that mechanism in the present. It's essential for us to understand these mechanisms because only in this way will we be able to make the best use of them. Otherwise, there's a chance these mechanisms can work against us. For a response to be triggered inside you, there's always an external stressor that causes it. When we gain a complete understanding of the presence of these mechanisms, we can then focus on using them constructively.

The types of survival mechanisms that we possess include:

- Anger and frustration
- Fear
- Depression
- Anxiety
- Loneliness
- Guilt

Anger and Frustration

Anger is actually a byproduct of frustration. We all have goals we want to achieve. When we're faced with multiple setbacks during our journey, we often get frustrated. The outgrowth of frustration is anger. The reason why a person becomes angry depends on their environmental situation. There are many events that can trigger anger in a person.

When anger is triggered in an individual, it may cause them to react impulsively. Such reactions prevent the person from actively thinking about their feelings, so they end up making impulsive decisions. Anger may also cause a person give up midway in an endeavor. The key to managing this response is to understand the intensity of the emotion. If we want to control our anger, we first need to understand our emotional state.

Fight or Flight

Our DNA contains a mechanism known as the "fight-or-flight response." This allowed our ancestors to properly respond when they faced an environmental stressor such as a dangerous species of animal or other humans that seemed like a threat.

This natural survival mechanism still influences the modern mind today. The fight-or-flight response is associated with the impulsive reactions we have. Whenever we're exposed to perceived danger, the fight-or-flight response kicks in immediately—prior to our ability to think about the situation. The amygdala gets activated when we're exposed to some threat, and it signals the brain to release certain hormones that cause us to react in a certain way in that situation. The body is signaled to run away or try to fight. The way we respond to any situation is the result of which emotions are being triggered.

The Thinking Part of Your Brain

The thinking part of your brain is located in the frontal lobes. This is the part of the brain responsible for rational decisions and planning. This part of your brain makes you aware of your emotions, enabling you to respond in a logical way.

We're unable to control the response in the amygdala because it's an automatic. However, the response generated from the frontal lobes is under our conscious control. The responses generated by the amygdala and the frontal lobes actually work together. For instance, if you see a dangerous-looking dog coming toward you, your amygdala will indicate that you should run. At the same time, your frontal lobes will process the information that there's a dog you don't know in front of you, but it may not attack you.

The thinking part of our brain often gets hijacked by the emotional part of our brain. If we compare the world today with the past, it's easy to see that the physical threats of hundreds of years ago were way more prevalent than psychological threats. In the present, there are more psychological threats. This is the reason why the flight-or-fight mechanism was more beneficial for our ancestors than it may be for us.

How Emotional Hijacking Occurs

Part of the reason that emotional hijacking happens is because our brain releases certain hormones. These include the stress hormones adrenaline and cortisol, which signal your body to prepare for a challenging situation. After the hijacking has taken place, you might feel regretful or embarrassed about how you reacted.

How to Identify Triggers

You can identify your trigger response by activating your frontal lobes. The key here is to become conscious of the situation and then react intentionally to it. This means you need to become more present in the moment.

The first step in identifying the trigger is accepting that you feel stressed or threatened by some external factor. Then you need to become aware that your fight-or-flight response has been activated. Next, you deeply observe how your body is reacting to the situation.

The most important action for you to take is to become calm. Remind yourself that you can take control of what's happening, and that your initial reaction may not be the best one. Stress will hinder you from thinking clearly, so, when you're calm, you start thinking rationally and logically about the situation you're faced with. Just inhaling slowly once or twice is sometimes enough for you to become present in the moment.

In this way, you'll become more aware of the warning signs and your triggers. You'll start noticing when they're present. Our thinking impacts our perceptions. Our inner thoughts play a significant role in establishing how we feel, which, in turn, determines how we act.

The Role of Perceptions in How We Think

Perception refers to how we interpret stimuli such as people, things, or events. We constantly see things around us, and the real challenge is in how we perceive them. You construct your perceptions based on how you see the world. Your perceptions are primarily influenced by your beliefs, past experiences, and cultural upbringing. Our sensory receptors are responsible for collecting the information around us, but it's critical to be aware of our perceptions because they're the driving force behind our reactions.

Your perceptions subconsciously tell you what to look for and how to interpret what you see or hear. Different circumstances evoke different perceptions. For example, you may perceive your coworker to be lazy because he always arrives to work at 9:30 a.m. when the start time is 9 a.m. Suppose he has a child with a medical disorder that needs special attention that isn't available until 9 a.m.? What if he's made arrangements with your manager of which you're unaware? These types of perceptions can be dangerous if we don't have all the facts.

Thoughts Are Powerful

Your thoughts are the most powerful weapon that you possess. They can make you do wonders, and they can also work against you. How you think impacts everything you do in life.

Your thoughts are related to your emotions. It might seem like they're the same thing, but they're entirely distinct from each other. Your thoughts are the collection of your ideas, beliefs, and opinions. Your thoughts also determine your perspective. Thoughts may seem like they randomly come and go, but they're very much under our control.

Your brain has two aspects—the conscious dimension and the subconscious dimension. Your subconscious controls instinctive behaviors and automated regulation of bodily functions, and the conscious part of your mind consists of thoughts, memories, feelings, and wishes that we're aware of at any given moment. When thoughts are constantly repeated in our mind, they become beliefs. When you're aware of your thoughts and beliefs, you're able to use them in a powerful way.

It's a universal truth that we are what we think. If you think bigger, you can achieve bigger, and if you think small, you'll only achieve small things. Before NASA announced it would send Neil Armstrong into space, it began by envisioning and believing such a feat was possible. NASA was able bring this thought into reality and make history. Similarly, our thoughts impact everything around us, and we can achieve all our goals if we have the right mindset.

A common misconception is that we believe it's necessary to change our environment whenever we suffer a disappointment in life. However, if we really want to see a change in our lives, we must change what's on the inside. Transformation begins from within. Whatever you think directly influences how you feel, and it signals your body to react in a certain way. Your emotions, thoughts, and feelings are interconnected with each other.

The Interconnection

Your thoughts alone don't have much power. They become powerful when you start investing your attention in them. If you pay attention to positive thoughts, you generate positive emotions. On the other hand, if you pay attention to negative thoughts, you only trigger negative feelings and emotions.

For instance, if you're having a hard time accomplishing a particular task, you may start telling yourself that you're not capable of doing that task. This then impacts how you feel about yourself, and you end up losing your motivation.

33

You start self-sabotaging, and your body language also changes.

Instead of self-sabotaging, if you believe that you can accomplish the task, your mood is uplifted, and you'll automatically feel motivated.

This shows us that our thoughts trigger our emotional response. This results in us feeling stressed, fearful, angry, empowered, optimistic, etc.

Cognitive Distortions

Cognitive distortions are thought patterns that cause a person to view reality in an inaccurate way, which is usually negative. These are habitual errors in thinking. Cognitive distortions contribute to negative emotions and fuel destructive thinking patterns that are particularly disabling.

Studies show that 80 percent of our thoughts are

negative. When we have too many negative thoughts, these become entrenched in our consciousness and interfere with everything we do and feel.

Here are a few examples of cognitive distortions:

- "I just failed my math test. I'm not good at school. I might as well just drop out."
- "I have the worst luck in the world."
- "How do we know it would even work?"
- "I'm not a creative person."

Understanding these cognitive distortions gives us a chance to reprogram our minds. You can restructure your thinking through behavioral techniques, which we'll discuss in more detail later in this book.

CHAPTER 2 – EMOTIONS

We've been expressing our emotions since the day we were born. When we're little, we don't know precisely why we're experiencing something. If you've ever observed infants, you might have noticed that even before they're able to talk, they express whatever they're feeling through emotional display. This could be laughing, crying, cuddling, feeling irritated, and much more.

As we grow up, we become better at labeling our emotions. We know what we're feeling, but we're often unaware of why we're feeling that way. This chapter will explore the characterization of your emotions and how emotions are much more than just expressing your feelings.

Emotions inform of us the options for reacting to a particular situation by letting us know what we're experiencing in the moment. We experience emotions every day, and most of them come and go. However, some emotions stay with us, and they can impact our mood for the entire day.

One vital point to note is that there's no such thing as a bad or good emotion. The only thing we should be focused on is how we can manage these emotions. Every individual expresses emotion in a unique way. The key to learning how you can control your emotions depends on your ability to understand them.

What Are Emotions?

An emotion can be defined as an electrochemical

38

signal that flows throughout the body in a continuous cycle. Emotions are a response to our perceptions about the world. As you learned in the previous chapter, perceptions shape the way we think about the world. Every emotion is valid, and it tells us about ourselves.

We need to accept and affirm all our emotions, which most of us have a hard time doing. We can be quick to judge ourselves when it comes to expressing our feelings. Observing why you feel a certain way is more important than telling yourself you shouldn't feel that way.

Emotions and Mood

Emotions are different from moods. People often use these two words interchangeably, but they're not the same. Emotions may not last for an extended period of time; however, even if we only feel them for a few moments, they may have a lot of intensity. This is why they have such a strong impact. On the other hand, a mood is something we might not feel that intensely, but it remains for a longer time.

It's been discovered that there are six basic types of emotions that every human being experiences. You can experience more than one emotion simultaneously.

These six emotions are:

- Happiness
- Fear
- Disgust
- Anger
- Joy
- Sadness

Emotional Responses

The Subjective Response

How emotions are expressed is subjective. There's been much research on the topic of emotions, and researchers have concluded that all human beings

40

experience these six universal emotions, but how they express them is highly subjective.

It's easy for all of us to relate to these emotions. For instance, if you're waiting for your exam result, you might be anxious and excited at the same time. It's hard to identify one emotion only. Anger is the most prominent example of emotions to which we each respond subjectively. The nature and range of the anger you feel might not be the same as that of your sibling. Everyone experiences emotions differently. Sometimes emotions can co-exist with each other, and it's completely normal to respond to one emotion at a time.

The Physiological Response

Emotions can impact you physiologically. You might feel a sudden roll in your stomach, which indicates you're feeling anxious. You might get sweaty palms if you're nervous about something. Your autonomic nervous system is responsible for the way your body responds involuntarily to a

41

particular situation.

Your sympathetic nervous system controls the physiological responses when you're experiencing an emotion. This part of your system reacts to the flight-or-fight response that happens in your amygdala. The amygdala is the number one organ that's affected by anger.

The Behavioral Response

The final step that occurs when you express your emotions is your behavioral response. Many expressions of emotion are universal. For instance, a frown can indicate that someone is angry, and a smile can show that someone is happy.

It's common for human beings to make assumptions based on the expressions of others. However, being truly aware of our own and others' emotions is a trait that not many people possess. This is known as emotional awareness. It's imperative to be aware of your emotions so you can manage them efficiently. In emotional awareness, you recognize, accept, and respect your feelings without passing judgment.

Why Are Emotions Essential?

The elements mentioned previously play a critical role in understanding your emotions. As we've seen, our emotions impact how we make decisions and also determine our motivation to complete a particular task. Here are some of the reasons why emotions are essential in how you think or behave.

They enable you to take action

To accomplish anything in life, taking action is the most critical step. Your emotional responses enable you to perform well when it comes to taking action. For instance, if you have an important job interview, your emotions might make you anxious and nervous. This, in turn, might cause you to dedicate more time to preparing so you perform well at the job interview.

43

By experiencing these emotions, you were motivated to take action. In many other circumstances, we often take certain actions in the hope of achieving positive results.

They help us identify threats

Emotions can help us identify a dangerous situation. The natural-selection mechanism was introduced by Darwin, and part of this concept says that the more adaptive a living thing is to its emotions, the better the chances of its survival. If we're scared by something, our first instinct is to escape the threat that's causing the fear.

They facilitate social interactions

Humans are social animals. Wherever we are, we usually interact with other human beings. When you interact with others, you need to know how to behave appropriately. You need to understand and respect the way another person feels, and it's also essential to give some hints of what you're feeling. You either express this through your body language or by stating your feelings directly. This makes the people around you aware of what you're feeling, and they take action accordingly. Without emotions, you can never fully express your likes and dislikes.

They help us with decision making

Your emotions have a lot of impact when you're making any sort of decision. Whatever emotions you're feeling are reflected in the way in which you make decisions. There's a particular type of brain damage that can affect a person's ability to experience emotions. It's been proven through research that people who have this disability have a hard time making rational decisions.

Emotions engender empathy

Emotions also help you understand other people, and how you express your emotions to other people helps them understand your mood. Similarly, you can get to know more about how a person feels by closely observing their emotions.

45

This deep understanding of other people's emotions helps you build strong relationships with them.

Managing Emotions

There are a lot of ways in which we can tell how another person is feeling. The two most important are their body language and the way they express themselves. It could be in the way they're speaking or their facial expressions. Communication isn't always verbal; that's why we need to notice a person's facial expressions and body language. More than 80 percent of communication is non-verbal.

We need to understand that we can control our emotions. It isn't always necessary for our emotions to control us. Emotions benefit us in a lot of ways, but, at the same time, if they aren't appropriately addressed, they can have a negative impact on our mental health. Because there's a close link between our mental and physical health, our emotions impact our whole being. You should never judge your emotions because they don't determine who you are. They're just emotions, and they come and go. You can regulate them and take control over them. This is a choice that every individual has. You just need to become more aware of them.

Learn how to regulate yourself

Consciously regulating your emotions is the number-one step in managing them. When your emotions become overwhelming, this happens because the logical part of your brain gets hijacked by your emotional response. If you're experiencing an episode of emotional hijacking, you'll have trouble processing information.

When we're working under stressful conditions, our amygdala is strongly activated. It isn't always easy to understand what we're feeling and why we're feeling that way. For that reason, we need to maintain a state of awareness about our self. Here are some ways that will help you cope with your emotions and think more clearly.

Take a short breath

Sometimes, taking a short breath can do wonders for us. When we aren't thinking straight, we often stop breathing properly. When you pause and take a deep breath, this brings you more into the present moment. You become more aware of yourself and your surroundings.

Whenever you feel overwhelmed by your emotions, try taking a small breath. This brings you out of your head and into your body. If you don't take a short breath at that moment, your amygdala will be in charge of your reactions. When you're calmer, the thinking part of the brain—the prefrontal cortex—is activated.

Understand your emotions

Understanding our emotions is very important. It helps us know what we need and want or don't want, and it helps us build healthier relationships. Understanding our emotions can help us talk about feelings more clearly, resolve conflicts better, and move past problematic feelings more quickly.

Delay the conversation

You may not always be able to manage your emotions in certain situations. If you're having an interaction with someone that triggers strong emotions in the moment, take a short breath and remind yourself that you can always delay the conversation rather than reacting impulsively. When you intentionally delay your response, this also provides the other person time to think. When you do this, you refrain from saying something that you might regret later on.

Emotional Intelligence

Emotional awareness refers to being aware of your emotions. You need to be mindful of the things around you, but, more importantly, you need to be aware of your state of mind and how you feel. Only in this way will you be able to manage them properly.

Intelligence isn't only limited to the way you excel in your academic or work life. Emotional intelligence is equally important. It's gained worldwide recognition and, just as IQ (intelligence quotient) measures intelligence, emotional intelligence is measured as EQ (emotional quotient). On your journey to manage your anger, you need to increase your emotional intelligence as well.

Emotional intelligence is the ability to control, perceive, and evaluate your emotions. For years, we've heard we need to see things from other people's perspectives and to have empathy for others. This can be difficult if you aren't aware of your own stressors and ways in which you regulate yourself. Improving your emotional intelligence can help you handle your anger, empathize with others, build stronger relationships, and reach your goals.

Here are some ways for becoming more emotionally intelligent and aware of yourself:

Regain control of your feelings

This is the most important trait that emotionally intelligent people have. They're self-aware. As you become more aware of yourself, you'll become more emotionally aware. Carefully observe your body language and how you react to situations to see for yourself what triggers you the most.

Label your emotions

You need to acknowledge whatever you're feeling at that very moment. Don't think about your past or your future—just be aware of your present self. Are you stressed? Are you anxious? Whatever you feel, you need to acknowledge it. You need to focus on what's going on inside you.

Anger can sometimes mask other emotions such as embarrassment or shame. Your focus should be entirely on you. Label your emotions, but don't identify them as good or bad. Simply be aware of what you're feeling at that very moment. This can make it easier for you to quickly identify your feelings.

Reframe your thoughts

Your thoughts play a huge role in managing your emotions. How you perceive the events around you impacts your feelings. If you perceive the situation negatively, your emotions are more likely to be negative as well. Whenever you find yourself overthinking or dwelling on negative thoughts, ask yourself a simple question: "What would I tell a friend who was in this position?" This will allow you to think more logically.

Managing your emotions can seem overwhelming, especially if you're new to it. You need to believe that you do have the ability to do this. You can practice emotion-regulating skills at any time and in any situation.

Please don't neglect your emotions because they're valid and they're a part of you. Reframe your thoughts when it feels like your emotions are overtaking you. Once you start labeling your emotions, you'll get better at recognizing them in the future, which is the first step to managing them—even powerful ones like anger.

CHAPTER 3–WHAT IS ANGER?

Anger is an emotion that tells you something's wrong. It might signal that someone or something has interfered with your goals, disappointed you, or mistreated you in some way. Anger can make you feel like defending yourself, attacking, or getting revenge.

We all feel anger to varying degrees, but anger becomes a problem when its severity or frequency interferes with our mental health, legal standing, performance at work, or relationships.

Anger is said to be the most powerful emotion. For this very reason, it's easy to misunderstand it. Frustration, threat, and criticism are the three main things that trigger anger. We can feel mild anger at certain people's behavior or when things aren't going to plan. We may also get angry when we're feeling sad.

Your feelings, emotions, and mood are distinct from each other, but they're closely linked. Your emotional response might change the way you feel about things. Anger isn't only experienced in your mind; it also shows in your body language. You might have an increased heart rate or sweaty palms when you're angry.

You can often know if someone is angry by the way they speak or by reading their facial expression. Staring, clenching of fists, and frowning are just a few universal expressions that suggest a person is angry. However, some people are good at internalizing their anger rather than expressing it, so it's not always obvious.

When anger gets out of control, it can be very destructive. It can cause problems in your personal as well as your social and work life. It may feel that this outrageous emotion can burst out any time, and you might not be able to control it. You can't control the amount of anger you have, but you can control how you express it.

Anger Isn't a "Bad" Emotion

A lot of people have a misconception that anger is a negative emotion. Anger isn't a negative emotion in itself, although it can be intense at times. Anger can be a positive experience for us as well. It can motivate us to stand up for our rights when we feel we're facing injustice.

By transforming his anger, Martin Luther King, Jr. was able to spread his message of nonviolence and become an inspiration for many people. Anger and aggressive behavior aren't the same thing. Uncontrolled anger can become aggression or even violence. However, anger can be controlled so it never leads to violence.

Research has shown that our various emotions are interconnected. It's been determined that fear is the primary emotion that gives rise to all others. A few examples of the emotions that arise from fear are envy, disgust, and anger. When you're fearful of something or someone, after some time, you might feel angry at yourself for your cowardly behavior toward that person or thing.

Fear and anger are the two most similar emotions we have. They both generate the same response from our autonomic nervous system. The common factor between anger and fear is that they both involve conflict, regret, control, and purpose. Control significantly impacts both of these emotions. When people get scared, they feel a loss of control, which can create uncertainty and uneasiness.

The Different Types of Anger

Here are the different types of anger:

Repressed anger

Repressed feelings cause repressed anger. When we don't acknowledge our feelings directly and ignore them, this is repression. We may believe that if we ignore them, they'll eventually go away on their own. When we suppress our feelings and emotions for too long, they become more prominent. This often leads to rage and explosive behavior. Long-term effects of this type of anger can have adverse effects on our physical and mental health.

Righteous anger

This kind of anger is often related to political and religious beliefs. This type of anger isn't acceptable because it can escalate and possibly lead to violence.

Passive-aggressive anger

This is a type of anger in which we release our frustration and anger onto someone or something but in an indirect way. We continue to repress our anger, but it emerges in inappropriate situations and even against people who are closest to us. We don't admit our anger or set boundaries. Instead, we start mistreating other people, which makes them feel bad about themselves. We may start being cold to someone or ignore them altogether.

Rage

Anger and rage are similar in origin but different in degree. Anger becomes even more destructive when accompanied by rage. However, whether rage develops depends on how we use and handle our anger.

Rage is the highest level of anger, and it's often expressed physically. It causes adrenaline and other hormones associated with anger to surge.

The Difference Between Anger and Rage

Anger, in itself, isn't associated with shouting and violence. Anger gives us a sense that we need to take care of ourselves. It makes us more aware of our surroundings, and it decreases our chances of being manipulated. It provides us with protection and assurance. If we distinguish between these two, we see that anger alone isn't enough to result in physical violence.

Rage is different from anger because it's a highly destructive emotion that can make any situation potentially life-threatening. Anger can remain under our conscious control; rage, however, isn't under our control.

The inability to deal with anger healthily can cause us to feel more stress. As we know, our emotions are interlinked, so when we can't figure out what we're feeling, this can lead to rage, which means we end up "exploding" on someone or something.

61

Rage isn't only subject to the influence of external factors; it can also arise from our mental environment. When this happens, it's destructive to our personality, leading to self-sabotaging and feelings of hatred toward oneself. This internal, bottled-up rage can also manifest externally.

Some people who've experienced rage say it causes them to become a completely different person—someone who's lost complete control over themselves.

The Types of Rage

Here are the types of rage:

Borderline Personality

This type of anger is associated with people who have a borderline-personality disorder that makes them feel rejected or unwanted. An inability to control emotions is the number-one indicator of this type of disorder.

A person with this type of rage might never know when there's a sudden change in the emotions. For instance, they may be happy one moment and become angry the next. People who suffer from borderline rage often push away their loved ones because they believe those people might push them away in the future. They look at their actions later and often feel remorse, which can lead to depression.

Narcissist

In this type of rage, a narcissistic person expresses rage because they feel their self-worth is being attacked in some way. This can manifest as uncontrollable anger and lead to physical abuse. People who show this kind of rage tend to hurt other people on purpose.

Bipolar

Bipolar disorder can create its own unique form of rage. Someone with bipolar disorder suffers from a recurring cycle of mania and depression. Mania makes the person feel powerful and optimistic—sometimes to such an extent that they lose touch with reality. They may be impulsive and subjected to constantly racing thoughts. People in a manic state may display aggressive behavior and anger, and they may be unaware of the reason for it.

As mentioned before, there's always something that triggers our anger, and this varies from person to person. However, there are certain basic types of triggers that can cause anger.

The Causes of Anger

Certain causes of anger are commonly observed in most individuals. By gaining insight into these causes, we can better understand anger.

Unmet Needs - Threat to Safety

There are specific core necessities that every person requires to feel safe and happy in their life. These basic needs include food, water, shelter, rest, security, and safety. When those basic needs aren't satisfied, we can experience anger. This anger results from having to struggle to meet those needs to survive. The longer the deprivation lasts, the more desperate we are to fulfill those needs.

Unmet needs and threats to our safety are among the most common factors that cause individuals to feel anger. Unmet needs make us frustrated, because they cause us to feel hurt inside. Unmet needs include not feeling sufficiently loved or accepted.

Grief and Loss

Grief is a natural emotion that arises when we lose a loved one or we believe we might lose them soon. Pain is natural, and it's okay to feel pain. However, when grief takes over your life, this can put you in a vulnerable state. The death of a loved one is indescribably painful, and it doesn't easily go away.

Anger is one of the stages of the grief process. It is okay to feel angry at that point. You may feel you don't have any power, and you start questioning many things that make you feel helpless.

Anger might also arise because you feel you've been abandoned because the person you loved left you, and you feel that huge hole in your life. Another factor that contributes to this type of anger is an inability to accept that we've lost our loved one. Sadness and fear are also factors that contribute to anger associated with loss.

Boundaries Being Violated

When you're surrounded by toxic people in your life, it can feel like they are violating your boundaries. These people might be narcissistic or manipulative, and they're invading your space on purpose. Anyone around you can become toxic, and you might not be able to escape them. Types of boundaries include physical, financial, emotional, sexual, and time. We often feel that just by their presence in our life, toxic people are challenging our boundaries, and this makes us angry.

Everyone needs boundaries so they have the freedom and space to strengthen their spiritual and emotional growth. The problem is that setting boundaries can be equally as challenging as trying to prevent yourself from being violated. You may be fearful that the toxic person might become angry, and you might not be ready for their reaction. This can make you angry as well, because you might believe that you're weak and may not be able to take a stand for yourself.

Disappointment and Shattered expectations

People are quick to have expectations of other people. When they don't get the desired result from them, they feel sad and hurt. The disappointment that arises from shattered expectations can easily make people angry. When we're disappointed in someone we love, certain emotions can be exacerbated. When this happens continuously, it can cause resentment, blame, and, eventually, even rage.

It's hard to accept the reality of being disappointed, and this is why our emotions intensify. We don't acknowledge the sadness of the disappointment. We feel we didn't get what we were looking forward to, and a response of anger is how we cope with that. Anger leaves us thinking about what could've happened, and we continue to consciously denigrate the person who let us down.

Guilt and Shame

Shame arises when we critically look inside and pass harsh judgments on ourselves. We may have no control over the things we criticize ourselves for. This negative self-talk often has roots in our childhood. Maybe a person from our past criticized us and made us think we really are that type of person. When this shame impacts our sense of self, it becomes toxic.

This toxic shame is what causes anger to arise. When we feel we're small, we tend to believe we deserve less. This leads to extremely negative self-talk, which can become worse with time.

Anger can be also be used to cover up guilt and shame. This is because we react defensively when we're criticized or sometimes even when we receive constructive feedback. We use anger to divert attention away from the pain.

Lack of Forgiveness – Bitterness, Resentment, and Revenge

It's normal to get angry when we're hurt by someone we love and care for. We can also become confused and sad. When these hurtful incidents make us constantly think about the situation or the person who caused them, we can hold grudges and feel resentment toward that person.

69

This gives rise to more negative self-talk, and we get swallowed up by our bitterness. Forgiveness can be a tough thing for some people, but if we don't forgive the person we believe wronged us, this low-grade resentment can build into full-blown anger.

Vitamin Deficiency

When we don't provide our body with proper nourishment, this can affect the functioning of our mind. We've previously explored the close relationship between the body and mind. If there's a negative effect on our physical health, our mental health will also be negatively impacted.

A deficiency in vitamin B is associated with increased anger and irritability in individuals. This vitamin helps maintain a good emotional balance in our mind. This deficiency is caused by the lack of certain macronutrients in your diet.

Substance Abuse (Alcohol and Drugs)

When individuals face ongoing challenges in their lives, it can be hard for them to find a solution to their problems. This can make them sad, which may lead them to search for sources of happiness that might include abusing alcohol or drugs. In many cases, these substances are addictive, and withdrawal isn't easy. This temporary fix may provide relaxation and happiness for some time, but certain drugs and alcohol can also make an individual extremely angry and volatile, causing them to react aggressively in any given situation. A person may use alcohol thinking it suppresses their anger, but it actually makes it worse. People under the influence of drugs or alcohol have little ability to control anger or rage.

Unresolved Childhood Distress

Anger issues can start building in an individual from a really young age if they've faced trauma during childhood. Childhood is the most critical time of our life. This is when we learn about emotions and ways to cope with them. People who have a history of childhood trauma might not know how to effectively and healthily manage their anger because they never learned how to manage their emotions. This leads to even more disruptive behavior that causes the person to become angrier.

The reason why people use anger to cope with trauma goes back to the instincts we talked about previously. Individuals respond to pain and fear with anger, and this shifts their focus from trauma to anger. Anger that results from a particular trigger is more commonly seen in individuals who've been hurt by that same trigger earlier in their life.

These are some of the common causes of anger. Once we know the reasons for our anger, we can then acknowledge and accept it.

CHAPTER 4 - THE TRUE COST OF ANGER AND WHY YOU SHOULD CARE

Anger is an extremely powerful emotion that can affect us both physically and physiologically. Whenever we feel angry, we might think that expressing it will have negative consequence for us. This shouldn't be the case, because anger is meant to be released from our system.

Managing our anger is different from holding our anger in. When we hear the term "anger management," we may think this means not expressing our anger at all. Suppressing anger means holding it in; this is damaging for us, and it's one of the root causes of anxiety and depression. When anger isn't expressed appropriately, it can disrupt our relationships at every stage of our life. Anger can also lead to crime and physical and emotional abuse.

The Cost of Suppressing Anger

Many studies suggest that when we ignore our emotions, they can cause adverse mental and physical reactions. These reactions can be both short-term and long-term. According to research, it was observed that people who suppressed or ignored their emotions had a 30 to 70 percent greater chance of premature death and were more susceptible to diseases such as cancer. This indicates that suppressing our emotions can have long-term effects on our mental and physical health.

Repression of Emotions

Repression of emotions occurs when you avoid your emotions. You don't do it consciously; it just happens. The suppression of emotions is different from the repression of emotions. You suppress your emotions because you're aware of the damage they're causing you, but you don't know how to deal with them effectively.

This is why we believe that if we ignore uncomfortable emotions, they'll eventually resolve on their own. Actually, the opposite happens. When emotions aren't addressed healthily, and we leave them unacknowledged, this costs us on a social and personal level. It may affect our friendships, partners, family, and our energy to deal with things.

<u>The Physical Cost of Anger</u>

Uncontrolled anger can also cause us to become ill more often. This is because an excessive amount of anger weakens the body's immune system.

There was an experiment conducted that showed how anger impacts the immune system. In this study, a group of healthy people was asked to think about something that made them angry. Immunoglobin A is an antibody responsible for fighting infection. In this group of people, there was a six-hour dip observed in this antibody in their system after they were asked to think of something that caused them to feel anger.

The saying, "happy people live longer," is true. You're three times more likely to experience a stroke as a result of uncontrolled anger. An angry outburst can lead to internal bleeding of the brain, and it can also create a clot inside the brain. It can lead to the sudden development of an aneurysm. The most severe damage that anger causes is to your heart. It can put your heart health at risk because repressed anger causes heart damage. The repression of anger can also increase your risk of developing coronary disease.

Smoking is the leading cause of lung damage, but your lungs can also become weakened from anger episodes. An experiment was conducted that showed men who had high degrees of hostility and anger had lower lung capacity. This increased their chances of contracting a respiratory disease.

These experiments and research show us the hidden damage that anger can cause. In addition to harming us physically and physiologically, it also has social consequences.

The Social Cost of Anger

There are high social costs that can be attributed to anger. People who have high hostility rates are less likely to have healthy relationships with their family and friends. They also tend to have fewer friends. The reason for this is that they're angry all the time, and this makes other people feel scared of them.

Angry people are also more likely to become

depressed. Anger can make a person verbally and physically abusive, so there's always a chance that a hostile, angry person might physically or verbally abuse the people around them. Because extreme anger puts constants stress on relationships, this diminishes the likelihood of emotional intimacy.

Angry people often don't realize they can have a cynical attitude toward the people around them. Hostile people don't recognize that their words and actions can have a massive impact on other people.

In most situations, an angry verbal outburst isn't an appropriate response. You can't lash out at your boss at your workplace. Similarly, when you have public interactions, aggressive behavior may not be suitable, as it can make other people feel threatened and scared. Uncontrolled anger can impact your relationships at work as well as your social interactions.

Humans are meant to be social animals. We need support from other people to keep going in life. It's been proven through research that, to survive, it's essential for us to have social relationships with other people. This includes interacting with our family members, friends, people at work, etc.

When we have social support from other people, this improves the likelihood that we can overcome any problems we face related to our mental and physical health. We're less likely to get depressed when we're surrounded by a healthy social group.

Why You Should Invest Time and Energy in Learning How to Control Your Anger

If you have uncontrolled anger, you need to invest the time to work on managing it healthily. Anger management helps you recognize the frustrations and triggers that cause you to become aggressive. It enables you to express your needs in a healthy way so you can better control your emotions.

Whenever you feel frustrated and irritable, that's a form of anger. When anger evolves into rage, a person becomes infuriated and violent. People experience irritation and subtle anger up to ten times a day. If we don't manage our anger, it often escalates beyond our control. Anger can distort our emotions so we're not able to express our self adequately.

The real cost of anger is the threat of not being able to fully live our lives in a healthy way. It can be extremely destructive and impact every aspect of our life. It's best to manage your anger in a healthy way as soon as you become aware of the problem rather than allowing the anger to continue to control you.

How Anger Affects Your Decision Making

To accomplish anything in life, you must make critical decisions. Leaving your job, starting a business, and getting married are examples of

80

some of the decisions you might have to make in life. A sound mind is the most crucial component of decision-making.

Angry people are more likely to be pessimistic and put blame on other individuals. Anger also makes people take more risks without thinking about the consequences of their actions. We can't make a good critical decision if we're under a lot of stress. This is because, when we're under stress, our mind can't focus. This causes us to make irrational decisions. When we don't make the right decision, we decrease our chances of excelling in life. This is why it's always preferable to be mindful when you're making any decision.

The Benefits of Learning How to Control Your Anger

Here are some of the benefits of being in control of your anger:

- Controlling your anger will allow you to have more control of what you say and do.
- You'll have less conflict with people, which will result in healthy communication and better relationships.
- Your social life will improve.
- You'll always feel refreshed and calm when you know how to control your anger in a healthy way.
- You'll become aware of the triggers that cause you to become angry.
- You'll have a better understanding of how you can manage and deal with your feelings.
- You'll have more energy, and you can invest that energy into things that are important to you.
- You'll be more assertive and able to set clear boundaries.

These benefits are examples of the real change that can happen when anger management is part of your life. The things that make you feel alive are actually the people around you and your own self. When you're handicapped by anger and unable to function well, it shows in all aspects of your life.

The ability to control this anger is inside you. You can control what you feel and how you express it. The only thing you need to do is take action right away. If you believe you can do this, then you can do this, because your thoughts create your reality. You just need to believe in yourself. The next chapter will explain the different elements that make you angry in the first place.

A Short Message from the Author

Hey, are you enjoying the book? I'd love to hear your thoughts!

Many readers do not know how hard reviews are to come by, and how much they help an author.

I would be incredibly thankful if you could take just 60 seconds to write a brief review on Amazon, even if it's just a few sentences!

Thank you for taking the time to share your thoughts!

CHAPTER 5 – ASSESS YOUR ANGER

One of the critical points of proper anger management is recognizing the signs that indicate you're angry. Once you realize you're becoming angry, you start taking appropriate steps and actions that make you feel calm and relaxed. Anger is inside you, and the ability to manage it is also inside you. Anger management is the perfect middle ground that prevents you from becoming aggressive but doesn't force you to suppress your anger. It's a healthy strategy that can dramatically change your life.

85

As we've mentioned, common triggers that cause us to get angry include the damage caused by a traumatic experience that happened in our past or when we lose our patience. We might feel we're unwanted or we aren't being appreciated enough.

Anger management comprises different techniques and tools that can help you in managing your anger in an effective manner. However, before jumping into discussing this, you need to better understand why you get angry.

Assess Your Anger

Your susceptibility to anger is directly related to three things:

- Physical activity
- Physiological reaction
- Thoughts

Genetic variability is also a factor that contributes to the way you respond to the stimuli and situations around you. Some people don't respond

86

immediately to things that trigger their anger response, while others have an immediate response to triggering stimuli. These people tend to be quickly affected by the external factors they find annoying, and this can make them angry very easily.

It's been proven through research that listening to assaultive music with violent lyrics can also contribute to making people more prone to anger. Similarly, playing extreme video games that are centered on killing opponents is also another factor that can stimulate anger. Humans are said to adaptive, which is why they're susceptible and reactive to stimuli in their environment. These responses include physical reactions when we're extremely angry such as throwing objects or punching the wall.

Assessing your anger means you're trying to understand it so you can control it in a healthy way.

Evaluate Yourself

There's no such thing as a perfect person. We all have our strengths and weaknesses. Our strengths make us feel empowered and more confident. These include our skills and the way in which we manage things. On the other hand, without our weaknesses, we can never truly know our strengths. Honestly evaluating yourself is an important part of your life when you're trying to make improvements. Evaluating yourself allows you to discover your strengths and weaknesses. You acknowledge these and actively address them.

If, in your evaluation, you discover you have a great deal of anger, you need to ask yourself whether your anger is your friend or your enemy. You can do this by evaluating the impact your anger has on you and your environment. If you're prone to anger because you're in an unhealthy situation or you feel someone's rights are being violated, your anger might not be your enemy. Your anger might help you cope with that situation or even help someone else. However, sometimes when you find yourself in a position like this, it's better for you to change your environment. You may take a stand for yourself because your evaluation has made you realize you're not in the right environment.

If you feel your anger is causing some serious distress to you and the people around you, anger isn't your friend. Another way to determine if anger is your friend is to observe whether you regret the consequences of your anger. The thing is, even though your anger might seem to be a weakness or an enemy, it's necessary to remind yourself that you need to get to know it in any case.

Now that you understand your relationship to your anger, it's time for you to think deeply about the origins of this anger. This may take some time, but you'll definitely find an answer. It's often said that the best way to manage your anger is by paying attention to your environment. There could be many reasons that you feel angry, and you also have the ability to use your anger to do work for good causes.

You can achieve your goals by using your emotions in the right way. The way in which you were raised plays a role in your anger. Individuals who've seen extreme violence in their childhood sometimes grow up to believe this kind of behavior is socially acceptable. Observing violence plays a huge role in the development of aggression in a child.

You need to evaluate for yourself whether your attitude toward anger is related to your social network, group of friends, or any other social interactions. You need to find the root cause of that anger. Once you do find its origin, you can then begin to heal those wounds and identify your anger patterns.

How Do I Know if My Anger is a Problem?

Some common indications that your anger is a problem is when it:

- Happens frequently
- Is too intense
- Lasts too long
- Is uncontrollable
- Interferes with your relationships
- Interferes with work
- Escalates to physical or verbal abuse

A Simple Way to Notice Your Anger Patterns

Whenever our anger gets triggered by some external factor, our tendency is to react immediately to that situation. It might seem like the reaction is immediate, and we don't have any control over it, but the reality is, we can recognize our anger patterns before we act.

There are certain physical signs that can make us aware of our anger. You need to be aware of the signs that let you know your anger is starting to boil up. This can help you to manage your anger before it becomes explosive. Noticing what's going on in your body is the easiest way to discover your patterns.

Here are some of the ways your body might react to your feelings of anger:

You might feel like your face is becoming red—and it may, indeed, become red.

- You're clenching your jaw and hands.
- Your heartbeat is becoming faster.
- You're having trouble focusing or concentrating.
- It feels like there are knots in your stomach.
- You may feel a sudden headache.
- You may feel restless and start pacing.

- Your shoulders are tense.
- You feel flushed and hot.

How to quickly recognize your dominant anger personality

Keeping in mind the above-mentioned symptoms, you can learn to manage your anger. Most of the time, we don't even realize we're angry until we're fully enraged. This is why you need to observe your responses carefully. In that way, you'll know how you react to a particular situation. If you're aware of your physical responses to feeling anger, you can control your behavior.

Discover the cognitive distortions underlying your anger

Your brain seems to be the most trustworthy organ of your body. No matter what happens, you always know that your mind is the source of the solution. However, our brain becomes programmed over time with repetitive thoughts, and these are often negative self-talk that have nothing to do with reality.

It's important to understand our mind because, even if it's giving us good information, our perceptions make not allow us to recognize this. It's always good to give a second thought to whatever your brain is trying to communicate, because it's your mind that creates connections among your ideas, thoughts, actions, and perceived consequences. When there isn't a healthy relationship among these, problems can arise. These create what are known as cognitive distortions, which include irrational thoughts that you enforce on yourself. Aggressive behavior can be the result of the relationship among thoughts, beliefs, feelings, and memories accompanied by a physiological reaction to a perception of danger or a threatening event.

This tells us that the way in which we perceive things plays a huge role in the way we respond to being angry.

Perception vs. Reality - Change the way you view situations

The way we process the external information around us has a strong influence on our tendency to engage in aggressive behavior. Violence is often driven by the misinterpretations we make during a particular social interaction. This attitude becomes habitual, and we begin to react to similar situations in the exact same way. We can't change the situation, but we can change the way in which we perceive that situation. Whenever you find yourself in a circumstance that quickly triggers your anger, always take a break and calmly reevaluate the situation.

Triggers

There are different triggers for each person depending on their life experiences. Because these can develop at a young age, there's a good chance your past experiences are associated with your

95

triggers. For instance, if you were bullied in school, it likely you'll be immediately triggered if you encounter someone who's excessively controlling.

Discover how people, places, and certain situations can activate angry feelings

Anger can't be excused by a stressful situation. However, knowing the way in which you'r affected by anger is the key to controlling your aggression. Take time to evaluate and to consider previous situations and your present situation so you can see for yourself what activities, places, people, situations, or time of day triggers angry feelings. Once you've identified your triggers, it becomes easier for you to avoid certain situations so your anger doesn't flare.

Some of the most common anger triggers include:

- Relationship disputes
- Being lied to
- Being disrespected
- Experiencing injustice
- Labeling, blaming, and shaming
- Violation of your personal space
- Constant disappointment
- Lack of control
- Abusive language
- Misinformation
- Specific individuals
- Money issues

Triggers and Negative thought patterns

Apart from external factors, negative thought patterns can also trigger anger. Whether anger arises depends on the way in which you interpret and think about a situation. Negative thoughts

97

easily provoke our anger.

These are some of the thinking patterns that can trigger anger:

- Mind reading – This refers to making assumptions and jumping to a conclusion without having all the facts, which includes assuming that you know exactly what a particular person is thinking about you. Or you believe that whatever harm a particular person caused you was intentional.
- Overgeneralization - When a person overgeneralizes, they take a single event and then inaccurately apply that conclusion to everything. This may include phrases like, "No one listens to me," or "Why do I always get interrupted during a conversation."
- Mental filtering - This is the tendency to ignore the positive and focus only on

the negative. You may intentionally reach for things that upset you, refuse to think anything positive, and start collecting minor negative things that build to the extent that you explode.

- Self-serving bias - This is the tendency to blame external forces when bad things happen and give yourself credit when good things happen. When you lose a sense of accountability, that's when angry feelings might be triggered. This usually occurs when you blame others for whatever problems you're facing and refuse to take accountability to fix them.

- Confirmation bias - This means favoring information that conforms to our existing beliefs and discounting evidence that doesn't.

- Catastrophizing - This type of thinking causes a person to dread or assume the worst when they face something unknown. This causes ordinary worries to escalate quickly into major fears. For example, you don't get a check that you were expecting, and you catastrophize that you'll never get it and, therefore, you won't be able to pay your rent or any of your bills and your family will be evicted.

- Personalization - This is the most common error in our thinking—which is, taking things personally when they aren't even connected to us at all. This distortion can come up when you blame yourself for a situation that isn't your fault or was out of your control.

- Labeling - This distortion is where people reduce themselves or others to a negative descriptor such as "a failure" or "a drunk." Labeling can make a person furious and cause some significant problems between people.

In summary, it doesn't matter if anger seems like an enemy because you can always work on yourself to make it your friend. Evaluation is the first step in finding your relationship with anger. Once you've found that, the next step is to identify the cognitive distortions that contribute to your anger. Lastly, triggers play a very important role in anger. You need to identify your specific triggers as part of your path to managing your anger.

CHAPTER 6 -EXPRESSING ANGER

Anger will eventually come out even if you try to hold it in. In fact, the longer you hold it, the greater the anger becomes. How anger comes out of you can be verbally or non-verbally. When anger comes out verbally, you might say certain words or phrases that you regret later on.

Whereas when you express anger non-verbally, you may cause violence which can end up causing harm to other people or yourself. You should never suppress your feelings because that only makes them more prominent and worse.

As mentioned earlier, the brain forms connections that are created from your thoughts and are expressed through your emotions. Expressing your anger is the stage of anger that can either benefit you or be destructive. This chapter will help you find ways to express your anger healthily.

No matter where you are, communication is an essential aspect of society that is given importance in social interactions. For instance, although you have a resume, you still must go on an interview to get a job. Dealing with anger and trying to express it healthily can be overwhelming. It may seem like that, but you can easily find healthy ways to communicate.

Strategies to Communicating When Angry

The essence of communication is to be rational. Whenever you do any sort of communication, your emotions are involved in it. Effective communication may not always be easy, especially if your emotions are too overwhelming. Here are some of the strategies you need to have to communicate effectively when you are angry.

Change your narrative

Anger is a powerful emotion, so your thoughts and feelings are at an extreme during this time. It can result in harsh use of words, language, or even physical violence. During times like these, you need to replace these extreme thoughts with more balanced thoughts. Firstly, you need to accept that things did not go as you planned and then consider how you are feeling about it. You need to assure yourself that whatever happened was not that bad, and most importantly, you need to be kind to yourself.

Understand your anger

Whenever you feel like you are outraged, you need to pause and think about what is happening around you. Try thinking rationally about the situation. Take a close observation and assess what you are feeling. You need to then think about all the possible things that might have made you angry.

Let go of your expectations

We all set certain expectations with people and things because we want a particular outcome. It is essential to let go of these expectations as they can make you highly aggressive when things don't go as planned. You need to pause for a bit and then analyze your expectations again. You need to find out that whether those expectations are realistic or unrealistic. When you rethink your expectations, then you are less likely to respond with anger.

Listen to your body

As communication is done verbally and non-verbally, you must carefully observe what your body is trying to tell you. Whenever you are angry,

106

you also experience it in your body. You might listen to your heartbeat as it will get faster when you get mad. Similarly, your muscles may get tensed. These are some of the ways in which your body tries to communicate with you.

Do not bottle up your anger

Suppressing your anger only makes it worse. It will eventually come out no matter how hard you try to control it. Evidence suggests that holding your anger can cause a lot of health problems, such as an ulcer. You should never bottle up your feelings; instead, you should learn how to manage them efficiently. Suppressing your anger can also have adverse effects on your heart rate. According to a study, it was established that people who held their anger were more likely to get heart disease than the people who properly expressed their anger.

Smart Communication

Certain physiological factors can contribute to

107

how you react angrily to a situation. Your whole body reacts when you get angry. Your face reddens, your muscles become tense, and your blood pressure increases. This is why you need to find positive ways in which you can express your anger. The key here is to express your anger constructively. Smart communication is the best way to communicate constructively.

Here is how you can control your anger with smart and effective communication:

Pause before reacting

Whenever we are angry, we become irate, and we respond to the situation immediately and then jump to a conclusion without thinking. You need to listen carefully to what the other person is trying to tell you. You need to take some time out and think about the situation carefully. You can always take a break and come back to the situation.

Be empathic

Whenever you feel like you are getting angry at someone, you need to pause and think about the situation rationally. You need to understand the perspective of the other person. You need to make the other person aware that you care about them and do not intend to hurt their feelings. This will lessen the amount of tension, and it will motivate both of you to find a way to work through these emotions.

Assert yourself

You need to assert your feelings and needs clearly. Ensure that you don't sound harsh or aggressive in the process. It can affect how other people see you in a negative way. It would be best to consider what the other person is trying to communicate with you.

When you are in a conflict situation, it is important to address your needs, but it shouldn't be done to an extreme that can be damaging to

109

your relationship. You must be considerate about the feelings of other people. You need to state what has upset you and try finding out how the issue can be resolved.

Practice positive communication

Positive communication is the one in which you effectively explain whatever you are trying to say. The main focus of positive communication is that it includes all the healthy ways in which an individual should express what they are trying to convey. You should always listen carefully to what the other person is trying to say to you. Continually analyze and rethink your situation. You should never jump to conclusions and always listen carefully to the other person. Secondly, if you feel like your anger is too much, then take a break and get back to the person after calming yourself down.

The Yerkes-Dodson Curve

Anger gives you stress. You might have noticed

that there are certain tasks in which you perform exceptionally well when you are under pressure. In the scientific world, this is known as the Yerkes-Dodson Curve, and it is the relationship between performance and arousal levels. This phenomenon states that when your arousal levels increase, then it can make you perform exceptionally well in your tasks. However, the performance gets diminished when the arousal level becomes excessive.

A great example of this would be when you are taking an exam. The stress makes you extremely focused on your exam. It is the optimal level of stress. When this stress becomes too much, you lose your focus immediately, and it becomes hard for you to concentrate. This means that you can use your stress just enough to help you focus on your task but not too much that you lose your focus. A great way to do that is by being mindful of what you are doing.

Expressing your anger is done by effective communication. No matter where you are, communication plays a huge role. It can be hard to communicate when your emotions become too overwhelming. If you get angry easily, then it is vital for you to find positive ways to communicate with people so that you don't end up causing any kind of damage to yourself or the person you are trying to communicate with.

CHAPTER 7-ANGER MANAGEMENT

Anger management encompasses various tools that can help identify the signs of anger and handle triggers in a healthy way. It enables a person to recognize anger at an early stage and to express their needs while remaining calm and in control. Anger management doesn't involve suppressing or avoiding associated feelings. It is the perfect middle ground that helps you to control your anger healthily.

Anger management is an essential step when you

are trying to control your anger. You can use anger in a positive way in which you can get many benefits. Anger management is the ultimate way to improve your well-being.

In most cases, anger is caused by a lack of understanding about the situation. Utilizing anger management techniques increases your empathy which helps in understanding other people. You start seeing the other side of the story. Your perspective becomes broadened, and you become fully aware of the things that trigger you or cause you inconvenience.

Control Your Anger and Channel the Energy Towards Your Goals:

When we use anger in the right way, we open many new doors and opportunities for ourselves. Here are some of the ways you can turn your anger into success to accomplish all of your goals.

Channel

You need to direct your energy to any kind of task so that you can stop things from getting enraged in your mind. You need to focus your energy on things that leave a positive impact on your health and well-being. Your emotions should be centered around doing and achieving positive things in life. Develop an attitude of gratitude; find things that you are grateful for. Find your reasons for wanting to overcome your anger issues.

Plan

Although you may be dealing with anger issues, you still have purpose and goals. You can use this determination to the fullest by planning out your goals and objectives. Often, when we think about achieving success, we always want it to happen as quickly as possible. Success doesn't happen overnight, which is why it is essential for you to set goals and plan what you want to accomplish in your life.

Execute

Once you have your plan made, then the next thing is to execute your steps in it. Use anger as an energy boost. Anger naturally increases energy; however, the key is how you use that energy. Take your angry energy and attack your plan. You might find the energy boost from your anger helps you in unexpected ways.

Don't overthink

Overthinking is the main reason we end up stressing too much about things that are not relevant. We can end up being in a capsule of our own rage. Whenever you feel like working on something, don't overthink it. Just start. Make the best use of your motivation. You need to simply keep moving and try being more in the present.

The importance of being in the present has been discussing many times in this book. The art of being present is something we all possess, but we still are unaware of how to make the best use of it.

116

When you nourish your inside, that is when your outside flourishes. This is the main motive of these anger management strategies. The good thing is that you can practice these techniques anywhere and at any time of the day.

Forgive

Forgive yourself and anyone else involved. If you want to transform anger into positive energy, you have to forgive yourself. You have to accept the fact that we all make mistakes. Be accountable; take responsibility for the things you may have said or done. Forgiving someone else is one of the most challenging steps in positively using your anger. If you hold a grudge against another person, it will drain all your energy and create stress in your life. Negative energy will only attract more negativity in your life. Forgiving doesn't mean you have to like the person or be friends, but it will unload the burden of what the other person did or said to you.

Anger management strategies

This is the most critical part of your journey towards managing your anger. These strategies are meant to be practiced by any age group. Before you begin practicing these techniques, it is important to do it what an open mind.

Here are some tips and techniques that can help you in healthily managing your anger.

Pause before you speak

Whenever you are about to say something, you need to first take a break and give it a thought. This makes you think rationally about the situation in which you are in. When you react immediately to a situation that is when you tend to get explosive and say things that you regret later on. Similarly, you need to give a chance to others to do the same thing.

First, calm yourself, and then clearly express your anger

When you think clearly, this also gives you a chance to express yourself clearly. Once you have calmed yourself down, you need to express whatever frustration you have in a straightforward manner. The key here is to be assertive but not aggressive. State your concerns in a way that you don't hurt anyone around you.

Breathing exercises

These are the exercises that you can do anytime as they are highly convenient for everyone. Everyone has triggers, but you can always calm these triggers by performing breathing exercises. Breathing is something we all do naturally, but it is essential to do conscious breathing when you try to calm yourself down. In this way, you will reverse the symptoms of anger. Here is how you can do this breathing exercise:

- Anger begins to show its symptoms in your body. When you feel like your muscles are getting tense, or your anger will come out any second, then take some time out for yourself for at least 10 minutes and try breathing in a way that makes you calm and relaxes your body.

- Start with deep inhaling and then exhaling out slowly. You need to continue this at least three times.

- When you are inhaling, count to 4, and when you are exhaling, count to 6

- As you breathe, you need to closely observe the effect that it is giving to your body. You need to feel the air in passing going through your nostril all the way to your lungs and your body. Observe the movement of your ribs and your body, and then repeat the exercise. If you feel dizzy, then start breathing normally.

Mindfulness Meditation

Meditation is a natural and effective way to become aware of yourself. When you become aware of yourself, then you know how you can manage your emotions in a well-mannered way. Mindfulness is something that does not happen overnight; but instead, it takes some time to build in your system, and it shows in every stage of your life. Here are the mindfulness techniques that you need to adopt to cope with anger healthily.

- You need first to notice your physical sensations, which include your stomach, chest, and palms. You need to take a closer look at your heartbeat. If it's getting faster than usual, then it is a sign that your anger is rising.

- Then start breathing with the rhythm of your physical sensations. You need to count at least ten times while closing your eyes. It would be best if you observed the breath going inside your belly through your nose. You need to imagine that your breath is coming out of your hands and toes as you exhale.

- Embrace your anger. You are trying to understand your anger here. Do not label your feelings as good or bad. Anger may have caused a burning inside you, but breathing has also brought calmness and relaxation to your body.

- As you are breathing, examine your thoughts. Whatever thoughts you are having, you need to let them go one by one. If you find yourself struggling with letting go of your thoughts, try seeing your thoughts' relationship with your feelings. Remind yourself that you are the observer of your thoughts and emotions.

- Once you are done with this, it is always healthy to communicate your thoughts and emotions with other people.

Be Assertive & Set Boundaries

Anger management helps you in teaching appropriate and coordinated behavior, which helps in managing your emotions. Throughout this process, you are setting up boundaries that help you manage your emotions. It is crucial to set boundaries for yourself before other people do that for you. They might not do it intentionally but just to test how far they can get away with you. It is okay to disappoint sometimes. The disappointment here refers to not being a people pleaser at all times. You are setting up some boundaries because you are trying to protect yourself and your dignity. You should never believe that your assertiveness is hurting other people.

An assertive attitude is the best way to control your anger. Assertive statements are statements that are made in a straightforward and calm manner. You invest some time in your response, and you take great interest in it so that you can respond appropriately. You encourage to hear all that the other person has to say. Assertive people don't need anger; instead, they use conscious assertive techniques to become consistent with anger management. It is never late to assert yourself; you can start doing it from today!

For more information on how to become more assertive, you should check out my book: *"The Keys to Being Brilliantly Confident and More Assertive: A Vital Guide to Enhancing Your Communication Skills, Getting Rid of Anxiety, and Building Assertiveness."*

Cognitive Behavior Therapy

Cognitive Behavioural Therapy (CBT) is an innovative and effective approach to psychotherapy that has helped millions of people worldwide manage and overcome a wide range of issues related to unwanted thoughts, feelings, and behaviors. CBT is an evidence-based treatment that focuses on the relationship between thoughts, feelings, beliefs, and behaviors.

CBT is also effective for anger management. You gain a greater ability to control your impulses, and you get a great sense of accepting people. CBT's primary goal is to show clients how they can recognize, challenge, and shift the cognitive patterns that have them stuck in a rut of repeating the same self-destructive behaviors based on their fears and other concerns.

You will need to consult a specialist to conduct this behavioral therapy. Choosing a mental health professional that is right for you is an essential step in the process, and it is always good to do some research on clinicians in your area.

Seeking professional help

If you believe that your anger doesn't seem to be in your control and you need additional help, you should seek professional help. It is always best to see the credentials of a certified psychotherapist rather than surfing up the internet.

While this book's techniques can help you improve your levels of anger, some people will still need professional support to help push them toward their goals. Additionally, for some people, these issues may be related to their brain chemistry, which may require medication. To have a satisfactory recovery experience, you must take a holistic approach that ensures you achieve long-lasting results and can learn coping skills that will shape the rest of your life.

The key is to have a non-judgmental attitude towards all of your emotions. Most importantly, the strength to do this lies in you. You are capable of controlling your anger, and with a strong will and a sound mind, you will be able to manage your anger.

CHAPTER 8–HOW TO DEAL WITH ANGRY PEOPLE

Dealing with angry people can be equally overwhelming as dealing with anger as an emotion. When you understand why a person reacts in a certain way, it becomes easier for you to deal with them, especially if they live with you. This chapter will explain how you can deal with angry people in a beneficial way for you and the other person.

There is a difference between being angry and

having bad behavior. If you feel threatened by the anger of someone, then it is always better to trust what you believe about them. You can seek help from others and find ways to resolve the matter. If you cannot resolve an issue at that very moment, it is always better to leave the room immediately. If the other person seems to be totally out of control, then report the incident immediately.

Anger is an essential part of self-preservation. It involves self-defense instincts that help a person in recognizing the danger or threat around them. When dealing with someone abusive, you may need to use anger for self-preservation. This doesn't mean to cause violence. People who rarely get angry are less likely to stand for themselves. You must understand how you can properly express your anger.

Coping Strategies

Here are some of the coping strategies that you can use to deal with an angry person appropriately:

Do not respond with anger

Fight or flight response is a natural trait that humans have. When you get confronted by an angry person, this response can get triggered, making you angry. It is okay to be upset about it as it makes you feel under attack. However, before you respond, you need to take a deep breath and calm yourself.

Respond after you have calmed yourself. Monitor your emotions and make sure that you regulate them. If you find yourself getting extremely stressed or upset about the situation, then distract yourself and go for a walk. You can always communicate with the other person later when you feel better.

Identify the cause

You need to find out that why the person is angry in the first place. You can ask them questions that will help you in understanding their triggers. You need to encourage them and ask why they feel angry. You need to be empathetic towards them and try thinking from their perspective. Try using specific, clear statements and refrain from using generic phrases. Show that you are interested in resolving their situation.

Distance yourself emotionally

In many cases, the reason why someone is angry is not related to you. When you know that you are not the reason why the person is angry, it gives you a sense of relief, and you are less likely to get upset by it.

Once you have a better understanding of the situation, you can find ways to resolve the issue. Don't get defensive, as this can escalate the situation and make the other person feel angrier. You need to show them respect and understand that you are trying to work mutually with them to resolve the situation.

Distract them

You can help the person by diffusing their anger. This means that you need to find ways in which you can divert their focus onto something else. Distracting can decrease anger. It can be challenging for an angry person to shift their mood immediately when they are aggressive. Using humor by showing them a funny video or making a joke can be an excellent way to distract but try not to do it excessively as it can also annoy the person.

Communicate with them

You need to communicate with the angry person and tell them how you feel about their behavior. If you live with a person who has angry outbursts at times, you need to let them know how you feel so they take account of their behavior.

Do not use statements that involve "you"; instead, use the statements that include "I." For example, "I get distressed when you shout at me." You are trying to be assertive and respectful. Anger can be in relationships, workplaces, and in the home. You need to respond calmly and be mindful of your words and actions towards a person who is angry.

Try being as empathetic as you can. If you feel like the other person's emotions are getting out of control, then you need to find additional support.

CONCLUSION

Thank you for making it through to the end of the book; let's hope it was informative and able to provide you with all of the tools you need to achieve your goals to become a happier person in charge of your emotions.

Everyone has emotions. You feel them almost every day and every minute. Sometimes these emotions can get overwhelming, and it can feel like they are controlling you. Anger is an emotion of yours, and it is the most powerful emotion.

Humans are born with this emotion. The response that comes when you are angry is a 'fight or flight response. This usually happens when you are faced with danger or a threat.

Anger is not a bad emotion and can be used healthily. It plays an integral part in protecting your body. Without anger, you would not be able to take a stand for yourself. Anger alone is not violent, but when it escalates to rage, it can cause explosive behavior and cause hurt to other people. When that happens, then you end up saying and doing things that you regret later on. The good news is that all of this can be fixed, and you can take control of your anger and rage.

When we talk about controlling anger, it does not mean that you need to suppress your anger. When you bottle up your feelings, those feelings become more prominent, and they come out even stronger. Excessive anger is not ideal as it can have damaging effects on your body and your brain. You need to find the middle ground where you can experience anger but in an appropriate way that it doesn't cause harm or damage. The middle ground of anger is indeed anger management.

Anger management is the ultimate way to deal with anger healthily. A change begins from within, so you need to get to know more about yourself before jumping into anger management strategies. You need to evaluate yourself and find out your common stressors.

Everyone has triggers that make them extremely angry. Each individual is different, which is why there are different triggers for everyone. You need to find out your triggers so that you can work towards managing your anger. Most importantly, you need to embrace all of your emotions and acknowledge that they are a part of you and you do have control over them.

135

Self-belief is an essential part of your journey towards managing your anger. Your thoughts, emotions, and feelings are interconnected. You need to have positive thoughts, and you need to believe in yourself that you can control your emotions.

When you are trying to change your life, it is important to acknowledge that a change doesn't happen overnight. You must stay consistent with anger management. All you need to do is take it one step at a time and one day at a time, and everything else will fall in place.

This book has provided you with the tools that you need to overcome emotional and mental obstacles. It's not a quick-fix tool by any means, and it will require some work, but it can be done with the right mindset. As you start rewiring your brain, you will notice that happiness and positivity come more naturally.

Everybody's journey is going to be different. The tools you have learned in this book can help no matter what your situation is. The important thing is to make sure you pick what works best for you and be persistent.

One more thing

If you enjoyed this book and found it helpful, I'd be very grateful if you'd post a short review on Amazon. Your support does make a difference, and I read all the reviews personally so I can get your feedback and make this book even better. I love hearing from my readers, and I'd really appreciate it if you leave your honest feedback.

Thank you for reading!

Bonus Chapter

I would like to share a sneak peek into another one of my books that I think you will enjoy. The book is titled ***"How to Stop Being Negative, Angry, and Mean: Master Your Mind and Take Control of Your Life."***

Do you find yourself fighting negative thoughts and feelings every day? Do you wish there was something you could do to be more positive? Are you tired of being controlled by your emotions? If you answered Yes to any of these questions, then you are going to want to keep reading.

We've all felt sad, happy, angry, mad, disgusted, excited, and numb. It's normal for emotions to change throughout the day. What isn't normal is constantly feeling down or feeling like you have to force yourself to be happy. We shouldn't be pessimistic about everything because "somebody always lets me down." If you have used the statement, "if it weren't for bad luck, I'd have no luck at all," then you likely need help for negative self-talk. It's not okay to feel like you have no other options but to feel bad. You have the right to be happy, and you can learn how to be happy and more optimistic.

That's what this book is here to help you do. It's no easy feat to stop the thought processes you have had your entire life. It will take some work, but with the right tools, you can learn how to rewire your brain so that you are happier and healthier.

Enjoy this free chapter!

"Once you replace negative thoughts with positive ones, you'll start having positive results."
– Willie Nelson

All you have to do is look around the world and see that there is no shortage of negativity. This can make it extremely hard for a person who strives to be positive to make a positive impact on themselves and others. The truth of the matter is, we are all going to encounter negative circumstances and people throughout our lives. Unless we can learn how to manage these things effectively, we will forever remain prisoners in our lives instead of taking control of our own destiny. That's what this book is here to do.

Let me ask you something, how often over the last two weeks have you felt angry, out of control, or down? Hopefully, you haven't felt these things that often, but there is probably a good chance you have. If you hadn't, then you probably wouldn't be here right now. Just know, if these feelings are ever-present in your life, or at least feel as if they are, you are not alone. The good news is, those feelings can be transformed.

Everybody gets angry now and then, but some seem to stay angry, or at least get mad more often than others and lose control. This book will help you to get rid of that rage that often comes with anger. Additionally, this book will help people who are looking to have more control over their anger and emotions in general. These proven techniques can change your life forever. Just imagine not allowing your anger to take control of your life. When you use these techniques within the book, you will learn how to stop your anger in its tracks, and you will soon find that you are a much happier and positive person. You will know how to deal with your anger, instead of falling prey to it. You can use that energy to fulfill something in your life in a constructive way.

As an advocate for mental health, mindfulness,

and positivity, I have scoured many studies and techniques and applied them to my own life, to figure out what helps and what doesn't. This, along with the years of experience, I truly understand the importance of mindset and psychology, and the role they play in achieving a person's goals and how they cope with disappointment, change, and stress.

This book is for people who have tried many other techniques and methods to control the anger and negative thinking but failed. This book will teach you how to set yourself free. You will discover the reasons for your anger. Then you will find that those negative feelings lose the grip they have over you.

After reading through this book, you will find that you are more aware of the power you have always had. You will have steps that you can take to improve yourself, and skills to use to rewire your brain to reach a healthier mind. You will no longer be caught off-guard by the negative sides of life. Ultimately, What you THINK leads to how you FEEL, and What you FEEL leads to how you BEHAVE.

With my help and expertise, you will have the knowledge and skills you need to change your mindset and grow as a person. Now, I'm not telling you that the information I will provide you in this book is a magical cure-all pill for happiness, but it will help you to grow. This book is focused on helping you start your mental health journey.

The great thing is, the brain is malleable and can be changed. It also doesn't take a lot of tools to change the brain. All you need to do is be more aware of your internal dialogue and change it to something more positive and healthier. Why wait any longer? Let's get started and learn precisely how to be a more positive and happier person.

Emotions

145

Emotions and thoughts are related, and we can experience them at the same time, but they are very different. Let's look a bit closer to see exactly what they are.

It might help you if you think of emotions as an experience and flow of feelings like fear, anger, sadness, or joy. Emotions have an innate ability to be triggered by external or internal stimuli. External stimuli might be from watching a sad movie or seeing a friend suffer from a disease like cancer. Internal stimuli might happen when you remember something sad.

Even though emotions are universal, everyone is going to experience and respond to them differently. Some might struggle with figuring out which emotion they are experiencing.

Emotions are there to help us connect with others and to help create strong bonds socially. People who can build strong emotional ties and bonds become part of a community and are more likely to find protection and support that is needed to survive.

People all over the world will have different thoughts, opinions, beliefs, and ideas, but most people will have the same feelings.

What Can Influence Our Emotions?

Research has shown that emotions can be contagious. Humans have a tendency to mimic another person's outward state like when you pass someone in the grocery store, and they smile, you automatically smile back at them no matter what you might be feeling inward. Our outward state can affect our internal states, too, such as smiling could really make you feel happier.

Other factors that can influence emotions:

- Physical Conditions

147

Thyroid disorders, Alzheimer's, Multiple Sclerosis, Parkinson's Disease, strokes, brain tumors, and metabolic diseases like diabetes can cause someone's emotional responses to change drastically.

- Genetics

To get a bit more specific here, personality and brain structure, including one's self-control, can affect their emotional expression. Even though a person's genetics can't be changed, the brain is a completely different story. There are six definite "emotional styles" that get based on the structure of the brain, but we can reshape them with some practice.

- Cultural Beliefs and Traditions

These can affect how a person or group of people express their emotions. Some cultures deem it as "bad manners" if you express your emotions in ways that might not be considered appropriate and healthy in another culture.

The Things We Think Can Impact the Things We Feel

Emotions and thoughts have a huge effect on each other. Our thoughts can trigger an emotion. It can also help you look at the emotion. Let's say you have a job interview in a couple of days, and you might begin feeling a bit scared. You can tell yourself that what you are feeling isn't a realistic fear.

Additionally, the way we appraise and attend to our lives can have an impact on the way we feel. If you have a fear of dogs, you will probably be a bit more attentive to the dog who lives across the street from you. You watch them very closely when they begin approaching you. You automatically start feeling threatened, and this can lead to some emotional distress. Someone else sees the dog coming, and the view them as being friendly, and they have an entirely different emotional response about the same situation.

Can Emotions and Thoughts Be Changed?

We like believing that our emotions are just one more part of who we are, and they can't be changed. Research has shown that emotions are pliable. This means that they can be changed. Here are a few ways you can change them:

- By changing an external situation. For example, leaving an abusive partner.
- By changing your attention. For example, deciding to focus on a positive aspect of any given situation.
- By reframing the situation. For example, an upcoming test is an opportunity for you to learn and not an assessment of your worth.

The way you choose to live your life has massive power over how you feel each day. Specific kinds of mental training like positive thinking or mindfulness could affect how we look at the world and can help us feel happier, more resilient, and calmer. Other studies have found several other attitudes like kindness, gratitude, and forgiveness that can be practiced and cultivated (Lawson, n.d.).

Defense Mechanisms

Defense mechanisms are behaviors that people use to remove themselves from unpleasant thoughts, actions, or events. These are psychological strategies that might help you put distance between yourself and the unwanted feelings or threats like shame or guilt.

Sigmund Freud first proposed the psychoanalytic theory, and it has evolved with time and says behaviors like defense mechanisms aren't under our control. Most people will do them without even realizing they are using them.

Defense mechanisms are a natural, normal part of psychological development. Being able to identify the different types of defense mechanisms could help you with your future encounters and conversations.

There are several common defense mechanisms. Dozens have been found, but some get used a lot more than others. In many cases, these responses aren't under a person's control. This means you can't control "what you do when you do it." Here are the most common defense mechanisms:

- Denial

This is the most common defense mechanism. It happens when you won't accept facts or reality. You will block external circumstances or events from your mind so you won't have to deal with an emotional impact. You stay away from painful events or feelings.

This defense mechanism is the most widely one that is known, too. You will often hear the phrase: "They are in denial." This is understood to mean that a person is avoiding their reality despite what might be blatantly obvious to everyone else around them.

- Intellectualization

Any time you have been hit with a situation that is trying, you might decide to get rid of all the emotions from your responses and try to focus on just the facts. You might see someone use this strategy when someone loses a job, and they decide to spend their days making spreadsheets about leads and job opportunities.

- Compartmentalization

This happens when you separate your life into separate sectors. This might feel like you are protecting several elements about it.

Let's say you decided not to discuss your personal life at work, so you block off (compartmentalize) that part of your life. This lets you live your life without having to face the challenges or anxieties when you are in a specific mindset or setting.

- Reaction Formation

Anyone who uses this defense mechanism might see how they feel, but they decide to behave oppositely.

Anyone who reacts like this might feel they shouldn't ever express negative emotions like frustration or anger. Instead, they decide to respond in an extremely positive way.

- Sublimation or Redirection

This defense mechanism is thought of as a positive strategy. This is because the people who rely on it have decided to redirect their strong feelings or emotions into an activity or object that is safe and appropriate.

Rather than lashing out at an employee, you decide to funnel your frustration into exercise or kickboxing. You could also redirect or channel your feelings into sports, art, or music.

- Rationalization

Some people might try to explain their undesirable behaviors with a set of "facts." This lets them feel comfortable with the choice that they made, even if they know that it isn't right.

Let's say that a person gets turned down for a date. They may rationalize the situation by saying that they weren't attracted to the person anyway.

- Regression

If a person feels anxious or threatened, they might

unconsciously "escape" into an earlier time in their life.

This kind of defense mechanism might be seen more in younger children. If they experience loss or trauma, they might act like they are young again. They might even start sucking their thumb or wetting the bed.

It can happen with Adults also. Adults who have a hard time coping with behaviors or events might start sleeping with a favorite stuffed animal, chewing on pens or pencils, chain-smoking, overeating comfort foods. They might stop doing their daily activities because they feel too overwhelming.

- Displacement

This is when you direct strong frustrations and emotions toward an object or person that isn't threatening to you. This lets you satisfy your impulses to react, but you don't want to risk the consequences.

One good example is getting angry at your partner or child just because you had a rough day at work. Neither one is the cause of your strong emotions, but reacting to them won't bring as many repercussions as blowing up at your boss would.

- Projection

Some feelings or thoughts that you have about someone else might make you feel uncomfortable. If you project these feelings, you are misdirecting them to someone else.

For example, a bully may project their own feelings of vulnerability onto a smaller, weaker target.

- Repression

Irrational beliefs, painful memories, or unsavory thoughts might upset you. Rather than facing them, you might unconsciously decide to hide them, hoping you forget about them altogether.

This isn't saying that your memories are going to disappear. They might influence your behaviors, and they might impact your relationships in the future. You need to realize the impact that this defense mechanism is having on you.

How to Be the Boss of Your Emotions

Being able to express and experience emotions is very important. As a response that is felt in any given situation, emotions can play a huge part in how you react. If you are in tune with them, you will have access to some critical knowledge that can help with:

- Self-care
- Daily interactions
- Successful relationships
- Making decisions

Even though emotions can help you with your life each day, they could hurt your interpersonal relationships and emotional health when they begin feeling out of control.

Any emotion, including positive ones, can be intensified until it becomes hard to control. With some practice, you can rein them in. Research has suggested that having the skills to regulate your emotions has been linked to our well being. They also found a possible link between financial success and these skills; working on that part might pay off literally.

Here are some suggestions to help you get started:

- Know When To Show Emotions

There is a time and place for everything, and this includes intense emotions. Uncontrollably sobbing is a normal response to losing someone you love. Punching and screaming into your pillow may help relieve some of your tension and

159

anger when you get dumped.

Other situations need some restraint. It doesn't matter how frustrated you may be, screaming at your boss over cutting your hours isn't going to help.

You need to be mindful of where you are and the situation. This can help you know when it is fine to express your feelings or if you need to sit still and think about your feelings for some time.

- Breathe Deeply

There is a lot to be said for how powerful breath can be, whether you are so upset that you can't speak or if you are ridiculously happy. Slow down and pay attention to your breathing. Some deep breathing exercises could help you take a step back from the intense emotions and allow you to get grounded so you can avoid any extreme reactions.

The next time your emotions begin taking control:

- o Inhale slowly; deep breaths will come from your diaphragm and not the chest. It might help you to imagine your breath coming up from deep inside your belly.
- o Hold the breath for a three count and then exhale slowly.
- o Think about a mantra. Some find that repeating a mantra can be helpful, something simple like: "I am relaxed." "I am calm."

- Get Some Space

Putting some distance between you and your feelings could help you react to them reasonably. This distance could be physical, like walking away from a situation that upset you. You could distract yourself by creating some mental distance.

You don't ever want to avoid or block your feelings

completely, but it won't hurt you to distract yourself until you are in a place where you can deal with them better. Just be sure you come back to them. Any healthy distraction will just be temporary. You can try:

1. Spend time with your pet
2. Talk to someone you trust
3. Watch a funny video
4. Take a walk

- Get Control of Your Stress

If you are under a lot of stress, handling your emotions might be harder. People who are usually in control of their emotions might find it harder to handle them when they are under stress or a lot of tension.

Finding ways to manage your stress or reducing your stress might help you manage your emotions. Mindfulness practices such as meditation could help relieve stress, too. It isn't going to get rid of it entirely, but it could make it easier to deal with.

Here are some other ways to help you cope with stress:

1. Take time to do your hobbies
2. Take time to relax
3. Spend time in nature
4. Exercise
5. Make time to laugh and talk with close friends
6. Get an adequate amount of sleep

- Meditate

If you already practice meditation, this might be your best method for handling your extreme feelings. Meditation helps you increase your awareness of all your experiences and emotions. While meditating, you will be teaching yourself how to sit still with those feelings. You will be able to see them without making them go away, trying to change them, or judging yourself.

Learning to accept your emotions can make regulating them easier. Meditation can help increase these acceptance skills. It offers you other benefits, too, such as helping you sleep better and relaxing you.

- Keep a Journal

Writing about your feelings and the responses that they trigger could help you to identify patterns. There are times when it might be enough to trace those emotions back through those thoughts. Putting your feelings onto paper can let you reflect on them on a deeper level.

It can help you see when certain circumstances contribute to emotions that are harder to control. Finding those triggers can make it possible to find ways to manage them better.

Journaling can give you the best benefits when you do it each day. Keep it with you and write down any intense feelings or emotions when they happen. Make sure you write down the triggers and then how you reacted to it. If the reaction didn't help, write in your journal to find things that will be more helpful for your future.

- Accept All of Your Emotions

If you want to manage your emotions better, you could try downplaying your feelings. If you tend to collapse to the floor sobbing and to scream when you can't find your keys, or you hyperventilate when you get good news, it might help you to tell yourself: "It isn't a big deal, so stop freaking out." or "Just calm down."

This won't work. It is invalidating your experience because, to you, it is a huge deal. Accepting your emotions as they come up helps you become comfortable with them. When you can increase your comfort level around these intense emotions, it will let you feel them entirely without reacting in unhelpful or extreme ways.

165

To practice accepting your emotions, you can try thinking about them as messengers. They aren't bad or good. They are only neutral. They might bring up some unpleasant feelings every now and then, but they are still giving you information that you can use.

You could try something like:

"I am upset because I keep losing my keys, and this makes me late. I should put a dish on the shelf by the door, so I remember to leave them in the same place."

When you accept your emotions, you will be able to find more positivity and fewer mental health problems. This can lead to more happiness over all.

- Identify Your Feelings

Take a few minutes to check in about your mood. This can help you gain control. Let's say you have

166

been dating for a few months. You tried to plan a date last week, but they told you they didn't have the time. You texted them yesterday: "I'd like to see you soon. Can you meet this week?"

They respond 24 hours later: "Busy. Can't."

You get upset suddenly. Without thinking about what you are doing, you hurl your phone into the wall, knock over your trash can, and kick your chair, breaking your toe.

You can interrupt yourself by asking yourself these questions:

1. "What am I feeling right now?" furious, confused, or disappointed
2. "What happened to cause these feelings?" They ignored me without explaining why.
3. "Does this situation have a different explanation that makes sense?" They might have been stressed, sick, dealing with something that they don't want to explain

to you. They may be planning on telling you more later.

4. "What do I want to do about these feelings?" throw things, scream, text them back something rude.

5. "Is there a better way to cope with them?" Ask them if everything is fine. Ask them the next time they will be free. Get some exercise.

When you think about all the possible alternatives, you will be reframing your thoughts. This can help you change your extreme reactions.

It might take some time before you can turn it into a habit. With some practice, doing these steps in your head will get easier.

- Stop Repressing Try to Regulate

Your emotions don't have a dial. But just imagine that you were able to manage your emotions by turning a dial. You wouldn't put them on maximum all day long. You wouldn't turn them completely off either.

Any time you repress or suppress your emotions, you are keeping yourself from expressing and experiencing these feelings. This might happen consciously or unconsciously. Consciously would be a suppressed emotion; unconsciously would be a repressed emotion.

Either one of these can lead to physical or mental health problems like:

- o Substance abuse
- o Difficulty managing stress
- o Pain and muscle tension
- o Sleep problems
- o Depression
- o Anxiety

When you are learning to gain control over your emotions, be sure you aren't trying to sweep them under the rug. Healthily expressing your emotions involves finding a balance between no emotions and overwhelming emotions.

- Look at Your Emotional Impact

Having intense emotions isn't bad. Emotions can make your lives vibrant, unique, and exciting. Having strong feelings can show that we are embracing life fully, and we aren't suppressing normal reactions.

It is normal to experience some overwhelming feeling occasionally. If something great happens, if something terrible happens, if you feel like you have been missing out.

How will you know if there is a problem?

Any emotion that constantly gets out of hand could lead to:

- Emotional or physical outbursts

- o Using illegal substances to manage emotions
- o Problems at school or work
- o Hard time relating to other people
- o Friendship or relationship conflicts

Take the time to figure out how your emotions are affecting your daily life. This makes it easier to find your problem areas.

- Find a Therapist

If you have tried all the above tips and your emotions are still overwhelming you, it might be time to find professional support. Persistent or long-term mood swings and not being able to regulate your emotions have been linked to specific mental health problems, including bipolar disorder and borderline personality disorder. Problems controlling your emotions could relate to family problems, trauma, or other problems.

A therapist can offer judgment-free and compassionate support while you:

- o Practice reframing and challenging the feelings that cause you distress.
- o Learn how to play limited emotional expressions up or downplay intense feelings.
- o Address any severe mood swings
- o Look at all the factors that contribute to your inability to regulate your emotions

Intense emotions and mood swings could provoke unwanted or negative thoughts that could eventually trigger feelings of despair or hopelessness.

This cycle might lead to unhelpful methods of coping, such as self-harm or suicidal thoughts. If you start thinking about committing suicide, or have the urge to harm yourself, talk to someone you trust who could help you find some support immediately.

Get your full copy from Amazon today! ***"How to Stop Being Negative, Angry, and Mean: Master Your Mind and Take Control of Your Life."***

Printed in Great Britain
by Amazon

78845183R00099